Mandala
Serene Coloring Book

Copyright: Published in the United States by Nancy McCowan
Published January 2017
ISBN-13: 978-1542630504
ISBN-10: 1542630509

Thank you

www.ingramcontent.com/pod-product-compliance
Lightning Source LLC
Chambersburg PA
CBHW081556280526
45788CB00011B/3484